A Hot Day

by Lola M. Schaefer

Consulting Editor: Gail Saunders-Smith, Ph.D.

Consultant: Chris S. Orr, Certified Consulting
Meteorologist, American Meteorological Society

Pebble Books

an imprint of Capstone Press
Mankato, Minnesota

Pebble Books are published by Capstone Press
151 Good Counsel Drive, P.O. Box 669, Mankato, Minnesota 56002
http://www.capstone-press.com

Printed in the United States of America.

2 3 4 5 6 04 03 02 01 00

Library of Congress Cataloging-in-Publication Data
Schaefer, Lola M., 1950–
   A hot day / by Lola M. Schaefer.
   p. cm.—(What kind of day is it?)
   Summary: Photographs and simple text depict some things that people see and
do on a hot day.
   ISBN 0-7368-0403-X (hardcover)
   ISBN 0-7368-8621-4 (paperback)
   1. Summer—Juvenile literature. 2. Heat—Physiological effect—Juvenile
literature. [1. Summer. 2. Heat.] I. Title. II. Series.
   QB637.6.S344 2000
   551.5'25—dc21   99-12902
                                                                    CIP

Note to Parents and Teachers

The What Kind of Day Is It? series supports national science
standards for units on basic features of the earth. The series also
shows that short-term weather conditions can change daily. This
book describes and illustrates what happens on a hot day. The
photographs support early readers in understanding the text. The
repetition of words and phrases helps early readers learn new
words. This book also introduces early readers to subject-specific
vocabulary words, which are defined in the Words to Know section.
Early readers may need assistance to read some words and to use
the Table of Contents, Words to Know, Read More, Internet Sites,
and Index/Word List sections of the book.

Table of Contents

Today is a hot day.

The temperature is high on a hot day.

8

The sun shines
on a hot day.

Plants wilt
on a hot day.

Some animals pant
on a hot day.

People sweat
on a hot day.

People use fans
on a hot day.

People swim
on a hot day.

People rest in the shade
on a hot day.

Words to Know

pant—to breathe quickly with an open mouth; some animals pant to cool off.

shade—an area that is sheltered from sunlight; the air may feel cooler in shady areas.

temperature—the measure of how hot or cold something is; temperature is measured with a thermometer.

wilt—to droop; some plants lose water and bend over in heat.

Read More

Crews, Nina. *One Hot Summer Day.* New York: Greenwillow Books, 1995.

Powell, Jillian. *The Sun and Us.* Weather. Longmont, Colo.: Smart Apple Media, 1998.

Saunders-Smith, Gail. *Summer.* Seasons. Mankato, Minn.: Pebble Books, 1998.

Internet Sites

All about Swimming
http://members.aol.com/msdaizy/sports/swim.html

Observing Temperature
http://www.miamisci.org/hurricane/temperature.html

World Temperature Extremes
http://www.iinet.net.au/~jacob/worldtp.html

Index/Word List

Word Count: 61
Early-Intervention Level: 8

Editorial Credits

Martha E. H. Rustad, editor; Abby Bradford, Bradfordesign, Inc., cover designer; Heidi Schoof, photo researcher

Photo Credits

ColePhoto/Mark E. Gibson, 20
Index Stock Imagery, cover
Photophile/Bachman, 1; Mark E. Gibson, 4
Root Resources/Earl L. Kubis, 6; MacDonald Photography, 18
Transparencies, Inc./Jane Faircloth, 12; Billy E. Barnes, 16
Unicorn Stock Photos/Eric R. Berndt, 8; Martha McBride, 10
Visuals Unlimited/Mark S. Skalny, 14